CONTENTS

SELWYN HUGHES

CAN I REALLY KNOW
FULFILMENT?

First published 1994 by Kingsway Publications Ltd.
This edition 2002

Unless otherwise stated, biblical quotations are from the New
International Version © 1973, 1978, 1984 by the International
Bible Society.

ISBN 1-85345-235-1

Produced by CWR Creative Services
Design and typesetting by Simon Ray @ CWR Creative Services
Printed in Finland by WS Bookwell

INTRODUCTION

If you had everything you have ever longed for, lived in the most beautiful home and environment imaginable, possessed enough wealth which meant that you would never have to work again, were surrounded by people who loved you and respected you, would that make you fully and completely happy?

There are those who would respond to that question with an unequivocal "yes". But the strange thing is, those who have tasted and experienced a good deal of what life has to offer would respond with an unhesitating "no". They have learnt that possessions do not necessarily bring happiness. Possessions bring comfort, luxury, financial security and many other things. But they do not spell happiness.

For over forty–five years now, I have worked as a counsellor attempting to help people who are looking for a sympathetic heart and an objective mind as they struggle with life's problems. When reminiscing recently about many of the issues which had been discussed with me in the counselling room, I recalled that in almost every counselling session I had conducted, two or three questions seemed to be ever-present in people's minds. I did not notice their persistency at first, nor was I always aware of their urgency, but years of experience have conditioned me to expect them and be ready to address them. What are these oft-recurring questions? You might think they would be: "How do I get out of this difficulty?" or, "What steps should I have taken to avoid finding myself in this position?" But they were: "*How do I overcome my feelings of emptiness? Is there some point or purpose to my being here on the earth? Can you help me make sense of what is happening to me?*"

In this book I have tried to deal with these pivotal and important questions. As to whether or not I have been successful in doing so, you of course must be the judge. I can say, however, that I have seen many people's lives transformed as they have considered and adopted the suggestions outlined in the following pages. I hope you find them helpful too.

Selwyn Hughes

CHAPTER ONE

IS HAPPINESS REALLY POSSIBLE ON THIS EARTH?

We look at the fact that at the beginning of the twenty-first century there are more ways than ever to be happy, yet few people seem to be happy – *really* happy. "How seldom a face in repose," said one philosopher, "is a face of serene content." The question is raised as to why.

IS HAPPINESS REALLY POSSIBLE ON THIS EARTH?

"If I had the power to grant your deepest wish or desire, what would it be?" This was the question I put to David, a successful thirty-five-year-old businessman who had come to me for counselling. "Make me happy," was his reply. "That's not too much to ask, is it?"

My contact with people and their problems for many years has led me to believe that most people (perhaps seven out of ten) would respond to the question I put to David in a similar way. I am convinced that the large majority of people do not merely wish for happiness – they *yearn* for it. Indeed, many work hard at trying to make themselves happy. They spend large sums of money on self-help courses or books, undertake a complete change of lifestyle, master some new skill, all in an attempt to find that elusive quality called happiness.

Every normal person would like to be happy. Those who deny they have a longing for happiness, who enjoy being disagreeable and say they do not care what people think of them are considered to be somewhat odd. In such people there may have been some mishandling in childhood, or some major defeat in later life. They have a kink in their personalities, which causes others to avoid them. All normal persons want to be at peace within themselves and in happy and comfortable relationships with others.

It has often been pointed out that the age in which we live has provided us with more reasons for being happy than any other throughout human history. Comfortable, centrally-heated homes, well-designed cars, satellite television, supermarkets stocked with a variety of foods, holidays abroad and so on. Yet put the matter to a simple test. Stand at a busy street corner for five minutes and study the faces of the people who go by. Or sit in a train or bus and observe the expressions of your fellow passengers. Few look *really* happy. "How seldom a face in repose," said one philosopher, "is a face of serene content."

Why is it that something so sought-after seems so elusive? One author asks the question: "Is happiness, like eternal youth or perpetual motion, a goal that we are not meant to reach, no matter how hard we work for it? Is it possible for people to be happy, really happy?" My answer to that last question is this: Yes, it is possible for people to be happy, *but most are going about it the wrong way*.

Millions of people think that happiness depends on things like achievement, fame, wealth, success or power. Oscar Wilde is reported to have said: "In this world there are only two tragedies. One is not getting what one wants, and the other is getting it." He was making the point that no matter how hard we work at trying to be successful, wealthy or famous, it simply will not give us the happiness we yearn for deep down.

One of the things talked about by psychiatrists and psychologists in these modern times is what they call "the Imposter Phenomenon". The phrase is used to describe the feelings of those who, apparently successful, find inside themselves a deep and incredible sadness. It arises, so it seems, from the unconscious belief that their success is really undeserved and one day they will be seen by others for the frauds they really are.

They know the kind of security that comes from wealth and power, but not the inner security that buttresses the personality and acts like an anchor to the soul.

This is similar in some ways to another condition known to psychiatrists and psychologists – "Success Depression". I had heard about this syndrome long before I came across it in a person I once counselled. The man concerned had risen from poverty to build a large and prosperous business in the City of London, and at the moment when he should have been enjoying his success, he fell prey to deep depression. It took a long time to get at the root of what was bothering him, but eventually it was tracked down. It was the sadness of having completed a task and having no further horizons to reach out for; the melancholy of everything completed. I was reminded as we talked of Alexander the Great of whom it was said that he wept "when there were no more worlds to conquer".

We read about the magnificent homes and lifestyle of the rich, the famous and the successful and think that if we possessed all the things they possess we would be happy. It's not true. Success, power, prestige and riches bring some benefits and rewards – it would be foolish to argue otherwise – but seemingly they are powerless to quench the gnawing hunger that is there within every one of us for unalloyed happiness.

I have met many, especially in more recent years, who think that happiness depends on *good health* and *physical fitness*. The age through which are passing seems fitness mad. That health and fitness have some part to play in helping us feel good cannot be denied, but to reduce the whole question to the physical ignores the inter-relation of mind and body, and over-simplifies the complex reality that is a human being.

Then I know some who argue that happiness is a matter of *temperament*. The ancient Greeks had a theory that we are all born with a certain caste of mind that remains practically unmodified through the course of our lives. Some are sanguine (optimistic), some are phlegmatic (unemotional), some are choleric (hot-tempered) and some are melancholic (sad and reflective).

There are many modern-day theorists who hold to this view and say we are all in one or other of those categories – we are born that way and we can do nothing about it. The sanguine, so they say, have a better chance of being happy than anyone. If you are in one of the other groups . . . well too bad!

There is of course a modicum of truth in these ideas about temperament, but I would emphatically deny the suggestion that it explains everything about life. I know many phlegmatics who sparkle and melancholics who overflow with joy. There is a power at work in the world that is greater than temperament.

Still others explain the presence or absence of happiness in terms of *circumstances*. A businessman on his way up the ladder of success responded to my question: "How do you define happiness?" like this: "Happiness is a nice home, congenial work, an adequate income, a loving family, dependable friends, a pleasant environment and good health. When you have all these things, you then have happiness." To him, happiness depended on *things*.

There is a terrible attachment in almost every human heart and mind to things. Millions of people make it their chief aim in life to get things. In a sense it is natural for people to desire a better-paid job, a bigger house, or a more efficient car. We live in a material world and it is impossible (as we said) to be indifferent to the benefits that material things bring.

The body may not be the most important thing about a human being, but it must have its due. I am sure it hurts you as much as it hurts me to reflect on the fact that by the time you have finished reading this page, hundreds of children will have died because they did not have anything to put in their stomachs. Man cannot live by bread alone, but it is also true that in this world he cannot live without it.

We may have everything a material world can offer us, and still feel empty; that something is missing. An awareness of this sense of emptiness resonates throughout every section of life. I read some time ago the story of Boris Becker, the famous tennis player who came close to taking his own life through being overwhelmed by a sense of hopelessness and emptiness. Even though he was tremendously successful he felt something was missing:

> I had won Wimbledon twice before, once as the youngest player. I was rich. I had all the material possessions I needed: money, cars, women, everything . . . I know that this is a cliché. It's the old song of the movie and pop stars who commit suicide. They have everything, and yet they are so unhappy . . . I had no inner peace. I was a puppet on a string. [1]

Jack Higgins was a highly successful thriller writer and author of the best-selling book *The Eagle Has Landed*. Whilst at the top of his profession he was reported as having once been asked what, out of all the things he knew now, he would have liked to have known when he was a boy. This was his reply: "That when you get to the top, there's nothing there."

I talked to a United States publisher a few years ago and asked him the question: "What sells?" "Anything that has the word 'Winner' in it," he replied. "We just can't go wrong with a well-written book that tells people how to avoid being losers." I thought of all the people I knew who were "winners", but who had confided in me during a counselling session that it wasn't enough.

So powerful is the desire for happiness in some that they will engage in potentially dangerous activities in order to stimulate within themselves feelings that approximate to happiness. I was once asked to talk to a young man who was addicted to parachuting. His fiancée had told him that she would only marry him if he gave up this dangerous sport. He came to me to ask how he could overcome his addiction. "Why do you do it?" I asked. He looked at me with astonishment and replied: "Because it is only then that I feel really alive."

Is this, I wonder, why so many people turn to drugs, in an effort to rise above the emotional flatness of everyday living, and experience what it feels like to really sense some vitality in the soul? I have often wondered to myself if the teenager who shoplifts or steals cars, and the housewife who drifts into an extramarital affair may not be doing it just because they want to do something wicked and sinful. The motivation behind it all may be a desire to add excitement to an otherwise humdrum and boring life.

Real happiness is not determined by circumstances, success, wealth, fame, winning, a loving family, good friends, a comfortable home, fitness or temperament. It is *influenced* by them, perhaps even moulded by them, but it is not subject to them. The great secret must be sought elsewhere.

If things like fame, wealth, success, a loving family and friends do not in themselves provide us with happiness and inner contentment, then what can?

Throughout time philosophers and sages have struggled with this question and have come up with a variety of answers. Freud, for example, said that people are happy when they experience *pleasure*. Adler, a disciple of Freud, disagreed and claimed it was feeling a sense of *power* that gave people inner contentment. Abraham Maslow, another great twentieth-century thinker, believed that people were happy when they were *self-actualised* – when they are able to reach the full potential of their capabilities.

I think Victor Frankl, the Viennese psychiatrist, was nearest the mark when he said that what makes people truly happy is when their lives have *meaning*; the sense that there is more to life than just being alive, eating, drinking, sleeping, working, or having children.

Carl Jung, the eminent psychologist, bore down on this point too when he wrote:

About a third of my cases are suffering from no clinically definable neurosis, but from the senselessness and emptiness of their lives. *This can be described as the general neurosis of our time* [italics mine]. [2]

I often reflect on the story a friend of mine, a professor of counselling in an American university, told me some time ago. During his student days, a highly respected member of the faculty died and in the memorial service that was held for him one of the speakers said this: "Let us take a few minutes to reflect on the life of our friend and colleague before the winds of time cover over his footprints in the sand." My friend told me, "I sat there thinking to myself: 'Is this what life is all about – living, working, dying, and then . . . the winds of time covering up our footprints in the sand?'"

As far as we can tell, human beings are the only ones who can reflect on questions that relate to the meaning of our existence on this planet. Our dogs and cats stretch themselves out on our living room carpets and are seemingly oblivious to the vital questions about life and living that intrude upon us humans. One writer calls this ability we have to ask questions of ourselves a curse, meaning that if we weren't able to ask the important questions about life and living, we would not be faced with the difficulty of trying to answer them.

What are some of the questions that arise within us from time to time that urgently press for answers? Are they not the ones I referred to in my Introduction? What am I doing on this planet? Am I just here to ensure the propagation of the human species? When I die, do I just go out into oblivion? Is there some point to my existence? Would it matter to the world whether I had been here or not?

These questions are rarely discussed at cocktail parties! But they demand answers nevertheless. In another of his trenchant remarks, Jung suggests that if we do not face up to these questions and try to answer them, we will find ourselves sick, lonely and afraid.

It must be emphasised that the need for meaning and purpose is quite different from our biological needs. It is also different from what might be termed our psychological needs such as the need to be accepted as we are or the need to see ourselves as valuable and worthwhile. The need for meaning is a spiritual or religious need; that is to say, it is a thirst or a desire that exists at the very core of our being – our spirit.

Where do we turn to find information that will guide us towards the discovery of life's meaning? Will philosophy (the humanistic search for life's meaning) give us the answer? I think not. Philosophy has been facetiously described as "a blind man, in a dark room, looking for a black cat that isn't there". It might be unfair to leave philosophy with such a bad press, so let me say a word in its favour. Philosophy can be helpful in showing us how to frame our questions and what to ask about the universe. It gives a sharp cutting edge to questions, but I have to say it is not very good at coming up with answers.

Does psychology have the answer? Again, I have to say "No". Psychology and psychotherapy (unravelling the affairs of the soul) can be extremely helpful in showing us how to adjust to life, but they are powerless to unfold the meaning of life.

I like what Harold Kushner says about psychotherapy in his book *When All You've Ever Wanted Isn't Enough*:

> A skilled therapist can untangle some of the emotional knots into which we have tied ourselves. He can remove some of the obstacles to our being happy. He can make us less miserable, but he cannot make us happy. Psychology can teach us to be normal but we must look elsewhere for the help we need to become human. [3]

Psychology has been a pet theme of my life and I have had some training in this field, but whenever people come to me with their problems it is not psychology I use, but another source of wisdom. I share with people what no therapist, relying on psychology alone, can share – moral absolutes and definitions of living that are rooted in the oldest and wisest book in the universe.

What is that book? It is the collection of the Jewish and Christian writings that we refer to as the Bible. There are many books in the world that say good and wise things about life on planet earth, but the book that best unfolds the meaning of life and gives us the truest answers to guide us through this world is, in my opinion, the Bible.

The Bible consists of sixty-six books all bound together in one volume and is believed by millions to be the most inspired and authoritative book on the subject we are now considering, that of meaning and purpose. One of the books of the Bible, the Acts of the Apostles, uses an interesting phrase to describe the system we know as Christianity – "the Way" (Acts 9:2). Note the capital letter in "Way". This Way is not *a* way among others, but "*the* Way" – the Way unqualified.

The universe is so constructed that there is "the way" and "not-the-way". In chemistry, for example, H_2O produces water. You may not like that formula and may prefer to work with another one, but you will never produce water. Two parts of hydrogen and one of oxygen is the way and everything else is not the way.

There is a way to fly and there is not-the-way. Aviators tell us that they must obey the laws of flight and surrender to them – or else! Someone has put it like this: "There are no moral holidays in relation to science." You obey or break. You gain mastery only by obedience. Aviators did not invent the laws of flight or impose them on the universe; they discovered them.

When Kant, the philosopher, said: "Two things strike me with awe, the starry heavens above and the moral law within," he was simply saying that there is a way and not-the-way written into both. If you obey, you get results; if you disobey, you get consequences. We see this at work all around us. Some people know how to live. They run with the grain of the universe – and they get results in happy, harmonious living. Others work against the grain of the universe and all they get are consequences.

When Edison, the inventor of the light bulb, tried over eleven hundred times to invent a light bulb and failed, someone said to him: "Then you must have wasted your time." "Oh no," Edison replied. "I found out eleven hundred ways how not to do things." This is where the age we are passing through is at the present moment. We are finding out how not to do things; how not to live. We must come to terms with the nature of reality. There are some things that are "givens" – we don't produce them, they are there built into the nature of things. Meaning is one of them.

Happiness flows out of a sense of meaning. Discover what meaning your life has in this world and you will find happiness. If you go about it the other way by trying to find happiness, the chances are you will end up in disillusionment and despair. In other words, to find happiness you must forget it.

The search for happiness is in fact one of the chief sources of unhappiness. There are many things in life you can get only by working for them or working at them. For example, a thriving business, the mastery of a musical instrument, the earning of a degree, familiarity with another language. These must all be worked for and, other things being equal, success belongs to the one who works the hardest. Happiness, however, is not something you get by working at it; happiness is a by-product. If you pursue it for its own sake, it will elude you like the will-o'-the-wisp. It is not the way. But if you give up the chase and turn your attention to other things then it is more likely to come home and stay with you.

People talk about "making love". Actually it is a misnomer. You cannot *make* love. You can express love, you can pretend to love, you can talk about love, you can demonstrate love, you can regulate your openness to love, you can foster or retard its growth, but you cannot make love.

Dr W.E. Sangster puts it like this:

Men cannot tell us what love is; they have tried but they have only "darkened counsel with words". You cannot tell what it is yourself. If you have ever attempted to tell anyone why you so regard them, you have probably mentioned a few more or less obvious virtues that can be found in five out of any ten people you meet in the street and who excite in you only the very mildest admiration. You don't know; you probably finished up very lamely like the man in the song and said, "It's just your way . . ." And in the same way that you cannot explain its nature you cannot explain its origin. One thing is certain; you didn't make it, it just came. [4]

So it is with happiness. You cannot make it. She is a coquette. Follow her and she eludes you; turn from her and focus on something else, and you may win her. Set out with the express purpose of finding her and you are doomed to failure. But discover the meaning that lies behind your life, and happiness will come home to you.

This law of our being is not easily learned, but both psychology and the Bible are at one on this point. And the experience of millions confirms it also. Perhaps the best way to illustrate it is to think of what happens when you play a game of golf or tennis. The pleasure is proportionate to the degree in which you lose yourself in the game. If you stop during the middle of the game and attempt to analyse the degree of pleasure that you are experiencing, any enjoyment you feel will vanish. To *get* the pleasure, you must *forget* it. If we stop whatever we are doing to give ourselves up to pleasure then any happiness we experience immediately dissolves, for as I said earlier – it is a by-product.

We only get happiness as we set out to get something else.

CHAPTER TWO

WHY AM I SO THIRSTY?

What is this strange thirst that exists within every human being – the ache to find something that fully satisfies? Where does it come from? Why is it so difficult to identify, let alone quench? We will now examine the underlying reasons for this.

WHY AM I SO THIRSTY?

The search for meaning is one of the main themes of the Jewish and Christian Scriptures. In the Old Testament, men and women are seen trying to make sense of the world in which they lived. The message of their spiritual leaders was quite simply that unless they made a connection with God, their lives would not make sense and would have no controlling purpose. There is a way, a path to living, said the ancient sages; a way that is in harmony with the universe; a clear plan for living life as it was meant to be lived. The New Testament conveys a similar message: there is the Way and not-the-way.

In addition to being a counsellor I have also been a minister and have had charge of several churches. In my capacity as a minister I explained to people the teachings of the Bible and often (especially by those who were being introduced to the Bible for the first time) this question was raised: "What is the Bible really all about?" I would usually give them this answer: "It's all about how thirsty people can find water to satisfy their souls."

The theme of thirst stretches from one end of the Bible to the other. It is to be found in almost every section of the ancient documents. An Old Testament prophet by the name of Jeremiah, speaking on behalf of God, told the people the reason why their souls continued to be thirsty was because they were going in the wrong direction in an effort to slake their thirst. This is what he said:

My people have committed two sins: They have forsaken me, the spring of living water, and have dug their own cisterns, broken cisterns that cannot hold water (Jeremiah 2:13).

Isaiah, another of the Jewish prophets, cried out to the people on God's behalf one day when he saw the deep spiritual thirst of the people going unsatisfied:

Come, all you who are thirsty, come to the waters; and you who have no money, come, buy and eat! Come, buy wine and milk without money and without cost (Isaiah 55:1).

The New Testament also makes reference to the deep thirst that is resident in the human soul, and paramount among these references are the words of Jesus Christ Himself: "If anyone is thirsty, let him come to me and drink" (John 7:37).

I know this may be difficult for some to accept, but there is no way human beings can experience meaning on this earth if they leave out God. Leo Tolstoy, the famous Russian novelist, put it like this: "Within every one of us is a God shaped blank and nothing, other than God, can fill it." In this materialistic age in which we live people seem to overlook the fact that we were made *by* God and *for* God. And we are suffering greatly for that misunderstanding.

One psychologist with whom I strongly disagree is the humanist B.F. Skinner, who taught that there is little difference between an animal and a human being. Known as the father of behaviourism, Skinner reduced men and women to the position of robots or automatons, destroying both freedom and responsibility. In his book *Beyond Freedom and Dignity*, he clearly articulates the idea that there is no such thing as a soul and that men and women, like animals, are the products of their environment. This view, shared by many humanists, is in my opinion a dangerous one. Why dangerous? Because if we don't understand the purpose and design that lies behind something then we are apt to try and do with it things the designer never intended.

Prior to becoming a minister I was a mechanical engineer. During the early part of my apprenticeship I was taught the different uses for different tools and then left on my own for a few hours to apply the knowledge I had gained. Unfortunately, I had not given my whole attention to what had been said and when given the task of dismantling a small lathe that needed to be removed to another part of the workshop, I attempted to make a tool do what it was never intended to do – and finished up breaking it.

When I reported the fact to my supervisor and showed him the broken tool, he looked at me in astonishment and said: "Tell me what you did." I proceeded to show him how I had tried to separate two pieces of equipment with the tool and how when it wouldn't budge I pressed harder and harder until it broke. "Weren't you listening?" he said angrily. "You have just cost the company a couple of hundred pounds. The tool you were using was not designed for that purpose. Couldn't you see by its very shape and texture that is not what it is for?"

I never forgot my supervisor's words and they came back to me years later when I read these words by psychiatrist John White:

If we want to know what anything *is* we must ask what it is *for*. What is a bread knife? You could say it is a thin strip of steel, sharpened along the edge, and your statement would be accurate. But if you said nothing more, you'd have said very little. If on the other hand you said that a bread knife is something you cut bread with, you'd be getting nearer the heart of the matter. Our understanding of humanity will be at best sadly incomplete unless we see what we are [made] for? [5]

27

Take fish, for example. After years of observing these creatures we cannot help but conclude that fish were made to live and thrive in water. "Water," says one writer, "is the only element in which fish can find its fishiness, its identity as a fish, its fulfilment, its freedom." What then of human beings? What are human beings made for?

Behaviourists like B.F. Skinner say we are nothing more than a complex bundle of neuron pathways, or that deep inside our brains are the chemical memory patterns that tell us these are the appropriate ways to act and react. We don't really think, he says – we *think* we think. We don't decide anything either, for everything we do is predetermined by stimuli from the things that go on around us acting upon our nervous systems.

Some behaviourists and humanists (though not all) define human beings in terms of behaviour, but the Bible goes right to our essence and tells us we are made "in the image of God". The very first few pages of the Bible describe the creation of the first man and woman:

So God created man in his own image, in the image of God he created him; male and female he created them (Genesis 1:27).

The Scriptures tell us something about mankind that science can never tell us. Ask a scientist who has no religious perspective to define a human being and you will get a very limited answer. A zoologist might say we are the highest of the mammals. An anthropologist might respond by stating that we are just social entities. A psychoanalyst might see us as victims of family pressures. I must confess I have a problem with those who try to explain human beings in such reductionist terms because we are more than just physical beings or the product of our environment; we are spiritual beings also. Something reverberates inside us that can only be explained in terms that lie outside scientific observation. We are made, the Bible tells us, "in the image of God".

But what exactly does this mean, "the image of God"? It means quite simply that we *resemble* God in the way we have been put together. The Almighty paid the highest compliment He could ever pay to human beings when He made us like Himself. God is a rational being who thinks. So are we. God is a volitional being who chooses. So are we. God is an emotional being who feels. So are we.

But perhaps the most important word used in the Bible to describe God is the word "Spirit". The Hebrew word means "breath" and gives us a picture of movement, activity and creative energy. In a sense we too have that aspect of the Deity built into us. We too can create – create a child, a painting, a design, or even a house. The great difference, of course, between ourselves and God is that while He is what theologians describe as "non-dependent" (He depends on no one for the energy by which He functions), we on the other hand are entirely dependent beings. God can get along without us, but we can't get along without Him.

In the Judeo-Christian view, the glory of human beings lies in the fact that men and women are image-bearers who reflect the nature and essence of their Creator. Note how this "down from above" view of the Bible, as opposed to the "up from below" view of evolution, has a marked effect upon our thinking. Think of all the great hospitals you know which are named after saints: St Thomas's, St Bartholomew's, and a whole string of others. These hospitals are monuments to a high view of humanity. The men and women who founded these great institutions were powered by a concern that the sick and suffering had to be sheltered and helped because they were made *in the image of God*. They saw that human beings derived their importance from the fact that they had been created in God's image.

In one of his books, Malcolm Muggeridge writes about the impact made upon him by Mother Teresa of Calcutta. This remarkable woman dedicated her life to helping the sick and suffering who littered the streets of that great city. During one of the sessions he had with her he says:

> I raised the point as to whether in view of the commonly held view that there are too many people in India, it was really worthwhile trying to salvage a few abandoned children who might otherwise have been expected to die of neglect . . . It was a point, as I was to discover subsequently, so remote from her whole way of looking at life that she had difficulty in grasping it. The notion that there could be too many children was, to her, as inconceivable as suggesting that there are too many bluebells in the woods or stars in the sky … To suppose otherwise is to countenance a death wish. Either life is always and in all circumstances sacred, or intrinsically of no account. [6]

Perhaps no one understood more the implications of people being made in God's image than the writer C.S. Lewis. In *The Weight of Glory* he wrote:

> It is a serious thing to live in a society of possible gods and goddesses, to remember that the dullest and most uninteresting person you can talk to may one day be a creature, which, if you saw it now, you would be strongly tempted to worship, or else a horror and a corruption such as you may now meet, if at all, only in a nightmare. All day long we are in some degree helping each other to one or other of these destinations. It is in the light of these overwhelming

possibilities, it is with the awe and the circumspection proper
to them, that we should conduct all our dealings with one
another, all friendships, all loves, all play, all politics. *There are
no ordinary people*. You have never talked to a mere mortal
[italics mine]. [7]

The missing element in most of the people-helping systems of
today is the spiritual one. But people are essentially spiritual.
Psychiatrists, psychologists and therapists who fail to take into
account that men and women have a spiritual dimension to their
existence will never be able to help people reach the kind of
adjustment that their souls crave.

Part of being made in the image of God means that when the
Creator made us in the beginning, He put within us a thirst for
Himself which is too strong and powerful to be satisfied by
anything less than Himself. One of the legends originating from
the Western Isles of Scotland illustrates this point most
graphically. It concerns a sea king who greatly desired the
company of a human being. One day he heard in his cavern under
the sea a cry – a human cry – and rising to the surface he saw in
the distance a little child in a derelict boat. Just as he was about to
make for the vessel and take the child, a rescue party intervened
and he missed his prize. The legend goes on to say that as the rescue
party hitched a line to the boat and drew it away, the sea king
cupped his hand and threw into the heart of the child a little salt
wave and said as he submerged: "The child is mine. When it
grows the salt sea will call him and he will come home to me at last."

The legend ends with the account of how when the child grew up
he felt the call of the ocean in his blood and spent his life sailing the
high seas. He could not bear to spend even an hour on land. It is only

a story of course, but it enshrines the timeless truth that God has put into every human heart a desire for Himself, which though it may be hidden, ignored, overlaid or even denied . . . it cannot be removed.

So we were made with a thirst within us which no water of earth can satisfy; an ache within us which only God can assuage; a hunger unmet except by the food that comes from above. Philosophers and sages right from the beginning of time have noticed this phenomenon. In one of his dialogues, Plato (Gorgias 493 b–d) compares human beings to leaky jars. Somehow we are always unfulfilled. We may pour things into the containers of our lives, but for some reason they never seem to get filled. We are always partly empty, and for that reason we experience a profound awareness of a lack of fullness and happiness. Diogenes Allen says:

Those who have entered the void know they have encountered a distinctive hunger, or emptiness; nothing earthly satisfies it. [8]

There is always another river to cross in the search for human contentment and it can only be satisfied by something *personal*.

It was George Herbert who in his quaint poem *The Pulley* said that God made mankind with "a glass of blessings standing by" and poured the blessings on His creatures until only one was left in the glass. It was the blessing of inward rest. Then God stayed His hand. Concerned that having all things mankind would never seek God, the Creator said:

But let him keep the rest,
But keep them with repining restlessness.
Let him be rich and weary, that at last,
If goodness lead him not, yet weariness
May toss him to my breast. [9]

If contemplation of the goodness of God does not drive us to Him, perhaps weariness with the pleasures of the world will have the desired effect. Pleasures, beauty and personal relationships all seem to promise so much, and yet when we grasp them, we find that what we were seeking was not located in them, but lies beyond them. There is a divine dissatisfaction within human experience which prompts us to ask whether there is anything which may satisfy the human quest or fulfil the desires of the human heart.

Clearly in every one of us there is something that earth cannot satisfy – not even the best things of earth. The testimony of those who have gained many of the things we have listed – success, wealth, fame – is uniform. There still remains a hunger and a longing that nothing on earth can meet.

Human love is probably one of the most powerful and satisfying things one can experience on this planet. To love someone deeply and to have that love reciprocated is one of earth's greatest joys. Yet deep within our souls is something that not even the most loving wife, husband, or dearest friend can meet. What we long for at the core of our being simply isn't there in any earthly relationship. The sooner we realise this the better. Not to realise it means we might demand from those who are closest to us something they are not really able to provide. This is what kills relationships.

I said earlier that the Bible has one central theme – to help people connect with God who alone can meet our soul's deepest needs. I believe the issue of meaning is a religious one. A century ago (perhaps even half a century ago) the things I have been saying in this chapter were a constant theme in church pulpits of all denominations. They still are in many churches (particularly those with a strong and vigorous confidence in the Judeo-Christian Scriptures), but regrettably more and more of our

33

pulpits are becoming places where the truths of the Bible are being replaced by clever little talks on current events.

It is being said that people don't listen to preachers these days and that religion has been replaced by reason. Perhaps where preachers fail to convince, the psychiatrists may succeed. Listen again to Jung:

> During the past thirty years, people from all the civilised countries of the earth have consulted me ... Among all my patients in the second half of life – that is to say, over thirty-five – there has not been one whose problem in the last resort was not that of finding a religious outlook on life. It is safe to say that everyone of them fell ill because he had lost that which the living religions of every age have given to their followers, and none of them has really been healed who did not regain his religious outlook. [10]

Dr John White says that it became clear to him in his psychiatric practice that man is "homo religiosus". He was careful not to take advantage of his position as a physician to impose his own religious convictions on vulnerable patients, but deep down he knew that many of them had profound spiritual concerns which they longed to share with someone they could trust. He explains:

> People will always pay a price when that religious drive within them is stifled or frustrated. And in the wild potpourri of cults, new religions and the pop psychologies ... I see only evidence of people's hunger and thirst for a God they do not know. [11]

It makes sense that if the need for meaning is not a psychological one but a spiritual one, then it is to religion we must turn for the answers. To know happiness we must know meaning. And to know meaning we must know God. That's the truth of it. The Bible says that God has set eternity in our hearts.

The thesis of this book is quite simple – our souls are hungry for fame, comfort, wealth or power. Those rewards create almost as many problems as they solve. Our souls are hungry for happiness and meaning, and nothing can satisfy them until these are experienced. We can go on day after day, have earthly applauds and rewards, but the question we must answer is this: "Do they *mean* anything?" There is a kind of nourishment our souls crave, even as our bodies need food, sunshine and exercise.

Indeed, C.S. Lewis unfolds this theme in many of his books – the theme that success and pleasure do not fully satisfy. It is a theme, says Lewis, that has intrigued the great minds of the ages. Listen to how one of the Old Testament writers put it:

As the deer pants for streams of water, so my soul pants for you, O God. My soul thirsts for God, for the living God (Psalm 42:1–2).

I spread out my hands to you; my soul thirsts for you like a parched land (Psalm 143:6).

Clearly there are within every one of us longings and desires that can never be fully satisfied with earth. What are we longing for? Many words come to mind: meaning, joy, a sense of purpose and so on. Most of us go through life wondering whether the deepest longings of our heart will ever be satisfied. We must let these longings lead us to the source of satisfaction – the one and only place where meaning can be found. If we pull back from this call – these outstretched hands beckoning us towards reality – then we shall feel as estranged as orphans.

Even the most casual observer of life on this planet must recognise that earth does not satisfy us. It seems to satisfy the birds and the beasts; they eat their fill, lie back and are content. But it will not satisfy us. Human beings have immortality locked up within them, so don't, I implore you, be deceived into thinking that if you had more of this, or more of that, you would be completely satisfied. It is an illusion. In his poem *World Strangeness*, William Watson asks:

> In this house with starry dome
> Flowered with gemlike plains and seas
> Shall I never feel at home?
> Shall I never feel at ease? [12]

Never!

CHAPTER THREE

WHY WON'T THE PAIN GO AWAY?

An unsatisfied strong desire, like an unsatisfied deep thirst, is painful to experience. We examine why it is that the terrestrial remedies we use to cope with our pain do not work. Do we have to be resigned to a life of pain – or is there some other way?

WHY WON'T THE PAIN GO AWAY?

The wonderful novelist Walker Percy has one of his characters, a psychiatrist, say:

> I seldom give anxious people drugs. If you do, they may feel better for a while, but they never find out what the anxiety is trying to tell them. I much prefer to help them get to what is causing the ache than to dampen it down with medication. [13]

We said in the previous chapter that although human beings belong to the earth, there is a hunger in them which earth cannot satisfy. This need or hunger is hard to define (and sometimes embarrassing to confess), but it seems to throb within us even when we have experienced some of the world's finest things – success, fame, wealth, sensual pleasures and so on. This need, which can perhaps best be described as *a need for meaning* (or joy), is not like our biological or even our psychological needs; it is a *spiritual* one and for that reason cannot be fully satisfied by anything terrestrial.

The way in which many people (perhaps most) go about dealing with this relentless ache that throbs deep inside us is interesting. They simply pretend it isn't there. I am not a disciple of Freud and I find some of his ideas unacceptable, but he made a valid point when he said that much human behaviour is influenced by the effort to maximise pleasure and minimise pain. His theory helps to explain why it is that we crave the pleasurable things of life – they help alleviate the pain of not having our central hunger satisfied.

Simone Weil echoes this same point when (using the metaphor of hunger rather than thirst) she says:

> The danger is not lest the soul should doubt whether there is any bread, but lest by a lie, it should persuade itself that it is not hungry. It can only persuade itself of this by lying, for the reality of its hunger is not a belief, but a certainty. [14]

It is often easier to deny the ache for meaning and joy that lies at the core of our souls than to admit to it. Once we admit to it we allow the unquenched longings to come fully into awareness and the result is pain. This pain is similar in many ways to the discomfort we feel when an intense physical thirst goes unquenched. It requires great courage to be willing to feel and experience emotional and spiritual pain, for underlying it is a sense of deep disappointment; disappointment that up until now nothing or no one has been able to meet the deep longings of our soul.

We say to ourselves, albeit unconsciously, "If I allow my longings to come fully into awareness, how can I be sure they will be satisfied? They have not been fully satisfied up until now. How can I be sure that there is someone or something out there that can deal effectively with the deep ache of my soul?" This uncertainty – the fear of disappointment – causes many to deaden their longings. "Not wanting, not desiring," says a friend of mine, "is humanity's main means of survival."

The realisation that there is something deep within our beings which up until now has not been fully and effectively met is probably one of the most powerful existential moments of our whole existence. In facing that realisation, and allowing ourselves to feel the emotion that such a realisation produces, we experience something we would rather avoid. But, to put it bluntly, avoidance does not work.

What I call avoidance the psychologists describe in a much more dynamic way. The term they use is *denial*. A psychologist friend of mine claims that while denial has a positive role of helping to keep out of consciousness things that tend to disturb us or threaten us, when it comes to the issue of the relentless ache for meaning or joy, then denial is counter-productive. I asked him why, and this was his reply: "Denial pushes the ache underground where it produces an intolerable desire for other forms of satisfaction. It is much better to face reality, confront the disappointment and allow the ache to surface."

When it hurts too much to feel, the tendency is not to feel. Avoidance (or denial) pushes out of awareness the ache we *ought* to feel. Why *ought*? Because the more keenly we feel the ache and the disappointment associated with it – the disappointment that up until now nothing or no one has been able to satisfy – the more likely we are to turn to the source which can fully satisfy. Facing and feeling the pain that our deep yearnings produce in us is part of growing as a person; growing in our understanding of ourselves, of others and of our Creator. Any attempt to deaden the pain enables us to go through life without pain – but at what cost?

Two things happened to me some years ago that brought a good deal of pain into my life. First, after a happy marriage lasting thirty-five years, my wife fell prey to cancer and died. A few weeks later, after a sudden heart attack, my father died also. My doctor asked me if I would like some sedatives to help cope with the pain, but I refused; not because I am particularly brave or courageous, but because I have learned that an unwillingness to face and feel negative emotions will inevitably result in an inability to feel fully the positive ones.

There have been many writers who have drawn our attention to the fact that the more we insulate ourselves against pain, the more we insulate ourselves against joy. "The same nerve endings by which we experience pain," says one author, "are the ones by which we experience pleasure." Our nerve endings, he claimed, were originally designed for experiencing good feelings, but like everything in creation they also have the capacity for feeling the opposite. "That is why rape is such a horrible thing; it is a violation of what in the right situation can be a beautiful thing." We can only experience the fullness of our positive emotions when we open ourselves also to the negative ones. We can become so good at not feeling pain that we learn not to feel anything – excitement, love, hope, joy, awe. We become emotionally desensitised.

I have met many people during the course of my counselling experience who appear to live out the whole of their lives within a narrow emotional spectrum. They have very few moments when they feel elated, but then they have very few moments when they feel deeply sad. Life is lived on a dull, flat emotional plane with no peaks and no troughs; no experience of fulfilment, but no experience of devastation either. "These are the people," someone has said, "who live lives of quiet desperation."

Confronting the issues of the soul is painful, sometimes extremely painful, but in the facing of them lies the route to pure happiness and joy. I don't mean masochism – a perversion in which a person experiences pleasure while experiencing pain. What I am talking about here is as different from that as chalk is from cheese.

Why is it necessary to face and feel the pain that is in our soul? I can think of at least two reasons. First, pain is a messenger that tells us something is wrong. As Benjamin Franklin put it: "Those things that hurt, instruct." A leading reason for people to think about seeking help from either a doctor or a therapist is depression. What many people don't realise is that depression (depression not chemically based, that is) is a normal and basically healthy phenomenon.

M. Scott Peck, in his book *The Road Less Travelled*, under the chapter heading "The Healthiness of Depression", makes the point that many people get bogged down in life to such a degree that the patterns and strategies they adopt to hold themselves together, and which don't really work, need to be broken up. He says that the process of "giving up" begins as soon as the depressed person decides to ask for help. The act of deciding to seek counselling in itself represents a giving up of the self-image: "I'm not OK and I need assistance to understand why I'm not OK and how to become OK."

It's not easy in today's culture (especially for males) to admit, "I'm not OK," because it is frequently equated with "I'm weak, inadequate and unmasculine". But since it is important to grow, facing the issues of the soul is inevitable. Thus, says Scott Peck:

Depression is a normal and basically healthy phenomenon. It becomes abnormal or unhealthy only when something interferes with the giving up process, with the result that the depression is prolonged . . . [15]

Depression is a messenger from the unconscious that says, "something is wrong with the way you are living. Find it, *give it up* and you will be well again."

A second reason why it is necessary to face and feel the pain of the soul is that attempts to avoid pain lead to a diminishment of ourselves as people. No normal person enjoys pain, but when we learn the art of detachment so well that we can experience disturbing and difficult situations and not be emotionally affected by them, we are diminished. A part of our soul goes. When I try to avoid pain by closing my mind to the message it is bringing me, and rush around, go on a spending spree, turn up the volume on the radio or take a holiday, I become less of a person; less alive.

There are some people I know who protect themselves from disappointment by deciding that they don't want to be happy; that happiness is simply a mirage, an illusion. This too diminishes the soul. Take it from me, to be a person in this world means that you will feel pain, and to hide from that pain is an avoidance technique that leads to impoverishment of being.

The tendency to avoid the pain that arises within us is the primary basis for mental illness, according to M. Scott Peck:

> Since most of us have this tendency to a greater or lesser degree, most of us are mentally ill to a greater or lesser degree, lacking complete mental health. Some of us will go to quite extraordinary lengths to avoid our problems and the suffering they cause. [16]

In the succinctly elegant words of Carl Jung:

> Neurosis is always a substitute for legitimate suffering. But the substitute itself becomes ultimately the more painful than the legitimate suffering it was designed to avoid. [17]

To experience true pain, to touch it and feel it and understand its message, is an expression of what life is all about. To quote C.S. Lewis again:

God whispers to us in our pleasures, speaks in our conscience, but shouts in our pains; it is His megaphone to rouse a deaf world. [18]

I have often put the following question to people in the counselling room: "What do you do with the relentless spiritual ache that is inside you? How do you handle this deep-down hunger?" Tony, one of my counsellees, gave me this answer: "I stuff it down as deep inside me as I can. If I let myself want what I know my heart desperately longs for, it hurts. So I try to make it as numb as I can in the hope that it will not go on troubling me."

Tony, of course, is not alone in following this strategy to deal with the pain of his unmet spiritual hunger. Millions of others do it also. Not wanting, not longing, as I said earlier, is one of the main means of survival for many. The sad reality, however, is that it does help to maintain a certain equilibrium. But at what cost? The more successful this strategy becomes, the more we deaden our hearts to the Creator who alone can provide us with what we really long for.

When I explained something of this to Tony, he countered: "Are you saying that the pain I feel, which in my more honest and stronger moments I allow to surface, is *good*?" I replied: "It's not good to feel pain, but the message the pain is giving you is good. The pain is there because you are not feeling at home with God yet. And He uses that ache to inform us that not only are we far from home, but that He has come looking for us. For the soul to be alive is to feel pain, and to hide from pain is to make yourself less alive.

Hiding from pain helps us avoid the lesson that pain is bringing us. No one ever tells us that there are dangerous side-effects to the habit of turning to painkilling medications and one of them is our diminished ability to feel anything."

Years ago when I was doing a training course in counselling I was told that I would not be an effective counsellor unless I was willing to face my own personal pain, whatever that pain might be. "You will not be in a position to help others," I was told, "unless you are willing to face and feel the things that are going on inside you." One tutor went further and said: "Never move away from the pain until you have found out what it is telling you." I have found that to be good advice. Too often, as we have seen, if we discover something painful or uncomfortable in ourselves, either we pretend it doesn't hurt, or we throw ourselves into some activity, take a pill, go on a shopping spree, in an effort to make it go away. We treat the symptom but overlook the cause.

The pain that arises within us due to our disappointment at so far finding nothing that can ease the ache that is at the core of our being is telling us several things. It is telling us that our deep longings for happiness cannot be satisfied by things, by people or by places. We can derive some pleasure from all these sources, but they are powerless to quench the central ache that is resident in our souls. It is also telling us that we cannot find it in ourselves. However disappointing that sounds, it is at least direct and honest. Human effort alone is unequal to the task of fulfilling our inner beings. Physical fitness does not produce it. Striving to climb up the ladder of success does not do it. Left to ourselves we are chasing a dream.

It is a fallacy to believe that we have it within our own power to make ourselves happy. This is a popular approach with many of today's authors and psychotherapists. "The secret of happiness lies within you," say these modern-day dispensers of their nostrum for humanity's ills. But that is patently untrue, when we have seen that happiness remains so elusive. The secret of happiness (real happiness, that is) is not inside us; it comes from outside us.

Psychotherapy can help us face the fact that we live in a world of upset plans, disappointing relationships and unrealistic expectations, and it can teach us how to adjust to this world and be less frustrated by it. What it can't do, however, is whisper to us of a world we have never seen or tasted. It can teach us to be normal in the sense that the world sees normality, but we must look elsewhere for the help we need to be a whole person.

What is the conclusion of all this? If we believe that in order for life to be good we have to avoid pain, the danger is that we will become so good at not feeling pain that we will learn not to feel anything – not joy, not love, not anything. Not even awe. We will have mastered the art of detachment to such a degree that nothing will be able to reach us emotionally.

One of the most fascinating radio programmes ever to have been aired was Dr Anthony Clare's riveting series entitled *The Psychiatrist's Chair* on the BBC's Radio 4. One of the people he interviewed on his programme was the well-known "agony aunt" Claire Rayner. In the midst of the interview she broke down uncontrollably when Dr Clare gently pressed her on the subject of her unhappy childood. Claire Rayner had already expressed to Dr Clare that she did not wish to talk about her childhood memories, preferring as she put it "to leave them at the bottom of the pond".

Critics of that particular programme raised such questions as: "Why, when Claire Rayner had already expressed her disinclination to talk about her childhood, did Dr Clare not leave well alone and move on to something else?" and "Why, when she broke down and wept, did he not respect her pain and change direction?"

Dr Clare defends himself by saying that he believed deep down in her heart Claire Rayner wanted to talk about those things. He says it was not the first time she had been interviewed by him and on the previous occasion she had also used the image of "mud at the bottom of the pool", but kept him at bay so that the interview ended without him being any the wiser. Of that first interview he says: "I sensed that behind her jolly bonhomie and breathless reassurance lay darkness and pain." [19] When he invited her for the second time he believed that she knew he would once again ask her similar questions and that if she did not really want to talk about what distressed her she would not have accepted the invitation.

When pressed further on why he would seek to probe into her childhood and help her get in touch with those deep hurts and wounds that were beneath the surface, he says:

> I did feel and still do that, given Claire Rayner's occupation, which is to purvey advice, reassurance, solace, sympathy and support to the thousands who seek it from her, it was important to discover whether she really was the composed, controlled superwoman she occasionally personified. Is the childhood mud related to the adult caring, I ask? *I could have asked whether in examining other people's miseries, she repeatedly confronts and exorcises her own* [italics mine]. [20]

This last statement of Anthony Clare's is crucial because if we are unwilling to face our pain, then it can reverberate inside us, and without our realising it may influence every action, every decision and every relationship. Many people take the view that it is pointless to "dig up the past" and certainly in my own counselling encounters I do not make a point of this unless I feel the pain needs to be confronted because of its impact upon the present.

By the way, Claire Rayner's idea that talking about unhappy childhood experiences is comparable to the self-indulgent stirrings of a muddy pool is not uncommon among those who are engaged in the task of helping people with their problems. They say: "There's not much point in digging up the past if you can't do anything about it." These people are usually tough and matter-of-fact in their approach to people and give the impression that getting up and doing something about one's problems is far superior to talking about them. But rushing about and doing things can often be a substitute for quietly sitting down and taking a look at what is going on inside and what particular inner distress is motivating one's actions.

Because self-understanding and self-awareness mean a certain amount of discomfort and pain, most of us are apt to resist facing honestly the issues that go on in our soul. Of all those who go to a psychiatrist or psychotherapist, very few are initially looking on a conscious level for challenge or education in self-awareness. Most are simply looking for relief. When they realise they are going to be challenged as well as supported, many withdraw or are tempted to withdraw. Teaching them that real relief will only come through facing reality is a delicate, often lengthy and frequently unsuccessful task. This is why you will often hear a psychiatrist or counsellor saying to someone on the counselling team that even after a year the patient has not yet entered into therapy.

It is easy to say we ought to be honest, but not so easy to do it. The business of being really honest in all things is usually more difficult and painful than we realise. Any psychotherapist will tell you that the most difficult people to help are those who are convinced that the cause of their difficulty lies in external situations – the home, the office, other people and so on. It is never in them. They will ask the psychotherapist to affirm them in this appraisal and will often resist the suggestion that something going on in them is causing the unhappiness.

Of course it is not easy to be thoroughly open and honest. I am intrigued by the fact that many of the plays of men like William Inge, Tennesee Williams, Arthur Miller, Eugene O'Neil and so on show this difficulty with agonising unpleasantness. Usually the opening of one of these plays shows the common scenes of life. Then little by little, as ordinary people confront each other, painful tensions and conflicts come to light.

The agony in modern drama is invariably provided by the character's gradual self-realisation which develops as his or her illusions are destroyed. Self-awareness means agony, and we are all prone to resist such scrupulous honesty. We are like the little boy who cries because he has a splinter in his foot, but is too afraid for his father to remove it.

It is a mistake to overlook the fact that honesty can be challenging, but it is equally wrong to assume that being honest is a miserable and terrifying experience. On the contrary, when the issues that go on in the soul are faced, really faced, then real healing begins. Reality is hardly ever as bad as the fear of it.

The Scriptures encourage us to live our lives openly before God and others, avoiding self-deception and illusion. We cannot hide from God, so why do we even try?

Psalm 139 is a classic statement of our inability to hide from our Creator.

O Lord, you have searched me and you know me ... you perceive my thoughts from afar ... you are familiar with all my ways ... Where can I go from your Spirit? Where can I flee from your presence? (vv.1–3, 7)

What may seem terrifying to the psalmist as he admits and reflects on God's concern for his life, becomes a blanket of security which calls forth his concluding petition:

Search me, O God, and know my heart; test me and know my anxious thoughts. See if there is any offensive way in me, and lead me in the way everlasting (vv.23–24).

The soul can never function as it was designed to function unless there is complete honesty. But self-honesty does not come painlessly. Those who study the function of behaviour tell us that the reason we lie to others or ourselves is to avoid the pain that honesty might cause us. President Nixon's lying about Watergate was no more sophisticated or different in kind than that of a four-year-old boy who lies to his mother about how the lamp fell off the table. Both are an attempt to circumnavigate legitimate suffering. The healing of the soul is of such a major issue that we must not let anything stand in its way. There must be no evasions, subterfuges, or prevarications. Honesty really is the best policy.

I urge you to fight with every fibre of your being the temptation to avoid facing the demands that rise up from within your inner being. Be alert to the tendency we all have to deny reality. Being open to challenge is disturbing, but life, real life, cannot be found without experiencing some upheavals in the soul.

CHAPTER FOUR

DOESN'T DEATH END IT ALL?

One of the most painful issues we face in life is the matter of our finitude. Is life on earth all there is? Do we arrive on this planet and then disappear for ever? We examine the truth concerning the future and look at how we can be sure of life after death.

DOESN'T DEATH END IT ALL?

One of the most painful issues we human beings are called upon to face in this life is the matter of our finitude. The irreversible fact is that no matter how much we jog, take care of our health, watch our cholesterol levels, how many vitamins we take, or health foods we absorb – we are all going to die. "The statistics concerning death", said H.G. Wells, "are impressive. One out of every one will end up in the grave."

The very first funeral I ever conducted was in the little town of Llandeilo in West Wales. The five-year-old daughter of some friends of mine was struck down with poliomyelitis and within a few days was dead. I had prepared a sermon for the funeral, but I was unable to give it. I could not stop my tears from flowing, such was the depth of emotion surging within me. All I could do was read the words of the burial committal, say a prayer and then bring the service to an end. I apologised to the mother and father as soon as the funeral service was over for the fact that I was unable to present my prepared address, but they brushed my apology aside and said: "Please don't worry; your tears were more of a comfort to us than any words you might have said."

Some weeks later, however, when I had recovered, I addressed the congregation I was then pastoring on the subject of death. I don't think any sermon I have ever preached had such an impact upon people as that one. People told me afterwards it was one of the most helpful sermons they had ever listened to. The gist of what I said that Sunday I want to put before you now. I began my sermon like this: "Just after ten o'clock on the night of 14th April, 1912, a calamity took place on the high seas that still occupies our attention even today. It has been the subject of numerous books, thousands of magazine articles and several documentaries and films. I refer of course to the sinking of the *Titanic*. This carefully constructed vessel, the largest vessel then afloat and said to be virtually indestructible, crashed in mid-Atlantic into an iceberg and four hours later went to the bottom."

I then went on to tell the congregation about the many fascinating stories told by the few survivors concerning those last four hours. They spoke, for example, of the calmness of the captain, the courage of the bandsmen who played "Nearer my God to thee" as the ship was going down, and the incredible bravery of some of the women who preferred to drown with their husbands rather than make for safety in one of the lifeboats.

One story I heard that greatly intrigued me was that of an apparently wealthy woman who, having been allotted a place in one of the lifeboats, asked if she might run back to her stateroom to collect some valuables. She was given three minutes to do this and hurrying along the corridors, which by this time were tilting at a dangerous angle, she burst into her stateroom and looked around for the treasures she wanted to pick up.

Her gaze fell upon three bright objects on the dressing table and without any further consideration she snatched at them and raced back to take her place in the lifeboat. The people in the boat looked at her in astonishment, for in her hands she held not priceless jewels, but three oranges. That little incident is instructive. An hour before, it would have seemed incredible to that woman that she could have preferred three oranges to one small diamond. But death had boarded the *Titanic* and in one fell swoop had reversed all human values.

I went on to say that ever since I had become a minister I had noticed that the closer people came to death the less earthly things seemed to matter. I told them I was not afraid to die – and why. I explained that my religious perspectives gave me a view on death that made it non-threatening. I hastened to add that I did not *want* to die and I hoped that I would live to a ripe old age. But whenever death came I was ready for it. I had learned to live, and therefore I was not afraid to die.

In this generation the subject of death seems to preoccupy us more than at any other time in history. A relatively new discipline called thanatology (from the Greek *thanatos* meaning "death') has entered our language and our classrooms. David Dempsey, an author who writes frequently on religious subjects, sees this preoccupation with death by people who have no real spiritual interests in this way:

Our society has secularised life. In doing so it has removed death from its traditional religious context, the belief that it is part of a natural order of things. When death was viewed more theologically, when suffering itself was thought of as spiritually purifying, when men believed in some kind of after life, death was more acceptable. [21]

People all over the globe have different views about death. Materialists see death as complete annihilation. Bertrand Russell was of this opinion. He wrote before his death:

There is darkness without, and when I die, there will be darkness within. There is no splendour, no vastness anywhere, only triviality for a moment, and then nothing. [22]

Hindus and Buddhists see it as an opportunity for reincarnation. Terrorists see death as a reward for giving themselves to a cause. Many Shiite Muslims believe that for every infidel they kill they will have incomparable sexual pleasure in the after-life.

Of all the fears that haunt us in this life, none is so intimidating as the fear of death. The intimation of immortality brings with it deep anxiety. Dr W.E. Sangster, the famous Methodist pastor who once occupied the pulpit of Westminster Central Hall, London, said:

> The fear of death is as old as human life and as long as human life and as widespread as human life. Whoever takes it upon himself to write of the fear of death may have little new to say but he is speaking to a great need of mankind. [23]

When I sat down to analyse the fear of death I found that several things emerged. Its psychological root is quite simple to unearth – it is the other side of the instinct of self-preservation. If men and women did not fear death then suicide would be far more common. Most of the people who take their own lives are regarded to be of unsound mind because it is a natural thing for a sane person to fear death.

When the late O. Henry, the famous short story writer, found himself surrounded by the shadow of death, he said to his nurse, "Nurse, bring me a candle."

"A candle?" she said. "Why do you want a candle?"

"Because," he said, "I am afraid to go home in the dark."

Many people fear the path that leads out of this life because it seems so dark.

Why do we fear death so much? The most obvious reason is that it is the greatest and most final change. Loss of the familiar and entry into the unknown are recognised causes of anxiety. In my time I have entered the homes of many who were bereaved and tried to support them as they attempted to cope with the changes that the death of a loved one produced. "What shall we do with his toys?" "To whom shall we give her clothes?" "How do I face the late afternoons when I hear the children coming home from school and I know my son will never run in through the back door again?" At such times it takes great courage as well as time to rearrange our lives and face the agony of change.

I once heard a preacher say: "Whoever is afraid of change is afraid to grow and afraid to live." I thought to myself "And also afraid to die."

"Those who fear change surround themselves with the things that are exclusively theirs, clinging desperately to them, against the inevitable tugs of time, much the way a child clings to the blanket that has comforted him since the cradle," was the way I heard another preacher put it.

There is a view held by some that it is not dying that people are afraid of, but of never having lived; of coming to the end of our days here on earth with the feeling that we were never really alive; that we never understood what life was all about. St Paul, who was converted on the road to Damascus, put the Christian philosophy of death in one of the most succinct and telling sentences ever written: "For to me, to live is Christ and to die is gain" (Philippians 1:21). Paul was changed from a persecutor of Christians to one of the greatest proponents of Christianity who has ever lived. Most theologians agree that throughout the entire history of

Christianity no one had a more remarkable conversion than Paul. His whole outlook on life was changed. So much so that when it came to dying he had no problem – death was just another change for the better.

Rabindranath Tagore, the famous poet and author from Bombay, India, is not someone I would normally quote to underscore a Christian view of death, but his explanation of death being fulfilment rather than continuance is effectively expressed in this passage:

There are people who have a static concept of life and thus only long for a life after death since they are interested exclusively in continuance, but not in fulfilment; they are happy in the illusion that the things to which they got used will last forever. In their thought, they identify themselves fully with their usual environment and with all that they have collected. The necessity of leaving them all means death to them. They forget that the true meaning of life is to live beyond … the fruit sticks to the stem, the shell to the flesh, the flesh to the stone as long as the fruit is not ripe; as long as this is, it is not ready for further life development. [24]

Another reason we fear death is because of the physical pain or torment we might feel as we pass from this world to the next. This is a very real dread to many people. Perhaps they have suffered greatly themselves and know from bitter experience how pain can lacerate the flesh. Perhaps they have witnessed a dear one pass from this world after a distressing struggle. I discussed this issue with a doctor in St Thomas's Hospital, London, on one occasion and he told me that in his view the "agony of death" is felt much more by the family of those who sit with a dying loved one than with the one who is passing over. "Is there any proof of this?" I asked. "No," he replied, "it is not something I can prove, but it is observation, and not only mine but many others' also, that most people experience a natural numbness of nature that sweeps over the whole body and blunts the power to feel."

Sir Frederick Treeves, the eminent surgeon in *The Elephant Man* said:

> The last moments of life are more distressing to witness than endure. What is termed the "agony of death" concerns the watcher by the bedside rather than the being who is the subject of pity. A last illness may be long, wearisome and painful, but the closing moments of it are, as a rule, free from suffering. There may appear to be a terrible struggle at the end, but of this struggle the subject is unconscious. It is the onlooker who bears the misery of it. To the subject there is merely a moment. [25]

My wife had one of the healthiest attitudes to death I have ever come across. She told me on more than one occasion that she was unafraid to die, but nevertheless she feared the physical fact of dying. "Will there be much pain, I wonder?" she used to say when she knew that she suffered from terminal cancer. Fortunately, the beneficent power of the drugs she was given in her last hours ministered to her needs and she died, as far as I can tell, peacefully and free of pain.

Yet another reason why we fear death is the fear of judgment. Throughout time philosophers and poets have written of this great fear that resides in the human heart.

We ought not to make light of this matter, for the fear of judgment finds a witness in every conscience. It finds support also in the iron law of cause and effect and runs through all regulated life.

A strong calm confidence in the face of an imminent confrontation with God is perhaps the luxury of only the arrogantly self-deceived. Every honest and humble person ought to have some feelings of trepidation about encountering God after death, and no one ought to be self-confident at the prospect of meeting with their Maker.

I talked to a man recently who was involved in the Falklands War. He told me that when he and his fellow soldiers were on board ship en route to the Falklands, he noticed that the closer they got to the theatre of war, the larger the Sunday morning congregations grew. At first when they set out from Southampton it was just a handful who gathered for the usual Sunday services, but on the Sunday prior to engagement it was impossible to get everyone in. Sitting around with his friends on the final Sunday evening the conversation turned to death and the hereafter.

Someone asked him if he was afraid to die and his response was: "The answer is, 'Yes and no.' Yes I am afraid that I might die a slow and lingering death. I am afraid for my wife and children if the end for me comes here in the Falklands. But there is another sense in which I can say, 'No' because knowing God as I do and having a personal relationship with Him assures me that if I die I shall be with Him. And that is a prospect that I have no fear of. I leave this world for another." This led to a discussion on what happens after death and my friend told me that for each one it was the subject of future judgment that concerned them most. He was able to show them that the Christian faith has a complete answer to this and that the Bible makes it clear that no man or woman who knows God in a personal way need fear judgment. We shall say more about this in the next chapter.

This point came home very forcibly to me in a drama I once saw on television which depicted a man who died and found himself on the other side, standing in line along with hundreds of others. He was addressed by an apparently bored usher who told him he must enter either of two doors. The door on the right led to heaven, he was told, and the door on the left led to hell. "You mean, I can choose either one?" the man asked. "There is no judgment, no taking account of how I lived?"

"That's right," said the usher. "Now move along. People are dying and lining up behind you. Choose one and keep the line moving."

"But I want to confess. I want to come clean. I want to be judged," the man said.

"We don't have time for that," said the usher. "Just choose a door and move along."

The man chose to walk through the door on the left leading to hell. In the end we all want to be held accountable. We want to be judged and ultimately forgiven.

Dr Elizabeth Kubler-Ross has given the classic description of the coping patterns of patients who know their diagnosis is terminal. The Swiss-born psychiatrist, now herself deceased, was an extremely sensitive person who counselled hundreds of patients and their families over the issue of death and dying. It must be emphasised that not all go through these stages in the order they are given below. And some might move through more quickly than others.

According to Dr Kubler-Ross, the first stage a person goes through when they realise they are about to die is that of denial. Upon hearing the diagnosis the patient usually responds with a shocked, "No, not me!" Death may happen to others, but it just can't happen to me.

Next comes anger or resentment. This is the stage known as, "Why me?" Here, blame is usually projected onto others: the doctor, the nurse and of course God. Counsellors are taught the importance of accepting a person who reaches this stage and allowing the words uttered to go unjudged.

The third stage is bargaining. "Yes, me, but …". When they arrive here at this third level, people begin to pray prayers like this: "O God, if you allow me a few more years, I promise I will go to church and live for you." Or, "God, if you keep me alive to see my children grow up and leave school, I will give you no argument about when I should die."

The fourth stage is depression. Now the patient says, "Yes, me!" Once the fact of death and dying is accepted, it is not unusual for depression to set in. Some counsellors believe this type of depression is a natural defence that helps subdue the emotional feelings which if not muffled in this way might tear the personality apart.

Finally comes acceptance: "Take me!"

I heard one psychologist say that one of the reasons why we middle-aged and older people make so much of youth in today's society is because of our fear of death. We idolise young athletes, for example, fawn over them and cherish them because they are so much further removed from death than we are. He said also that we grow uncomfortable in the presence of those who are much older than ourselves because they remind us that one day we too will be there, and that just beyond old age lies the terrible spectre of death. As I am of a scientific disposition I always listen to people with an attentive but also critical mind, and as I considered the points he made I said to myself: "That could be true, but it might not be true. Some people might find those statements unconvincing." I think far more convincing arguments to show we have a morbid fear of death are our use of words and our use of humour.

Those who have their finger on the pulse of spiritual affairs tell us that here in the West the fear of judgment is not as common as it was in previous centuries. This might be because church attendance was much higher in the past than it is today, and people who went to church heard many sermons on the subject of death and how to prepare for future judgment. My own experience confirms this, but I have noticed that even in the lives of those who claim to have no religion, there seems to be a built-in fear of judgment.

One of the greatest studies on the subject of death, and which brings out the point I am making concerning our use of words relating to death, is *The Denial of Death* by Ernest Becker. He points out how time and time again modern westerners attempt to evade this issue of death by the way they use words. The subject of death is being sanitised in today's society, so much so that many hospitals (particularly in the United States) don't talk of dying, but of negative patient care. I read in one British magazine that a person had arrived at a hospital suffering from "a negative mortality response". Why they could not just say the person was "dead on arrival" I don't know. Are such euphemisms part of today's worldview concerning the subject of death?

Perhaps the world's most famous cemetery is Forest Lawn Memorial Park in Glendale, California. I have been there several times on my visits to the United States. Here the bodies of many famous movie stars lie, surrounded by rolling lawns, sparkling fountains and marble statues. The famous millionaire who established the Forest Lawn cemetery was the late Hubert Eaton. He said he wanted to erase all signs of death and mourning and everything associated with it. Death became "leave taking", a corpse "the loved one" who was cared for not by an undertaker but by a "cosmologist" who put the deceased to rest in a luxuriously furnished "slumber room".

The happiest people I know are those who have a healthy attitude towards death. The Christian faith gives us this without any shadow of doubt. Dr Arnold Nickleye, chief of psychiatric services at Harvard University, says that there are four things which make for a healthy personality. One, a clear sense of one's identity; that is, knowing who one is and being comfortable with that. Two, a loving spirit that reaches out to others. Three, a sensitive conscience that can differentiate between right and wrong. And four, a readiness to meet death.

The famous author John Donne who lived in the seventeenth century wrote many wonderful things, among which is the celebrated passage which begins: "No man is an island unto himself." In 1623 John Donne was diagnosed as having contracted the bubonic plague and one day, as he lay desperately sick, he heard through his open window the church bells tolling out a declaration of death. He thought for a moment that his friends, knowing his condition, had ordered the bells to be rung in connection with his death, but after a few moments' reflection he realised they were being rung to mark the decease of a neighbour who had died from the plague. It struck him that although the bells had been sounded in honour of a neighbour's death, they served as a stark reminder of what every one of us on this earth would like to forget – we will all die. It was just after this that he wrote the immortal words: "Never send to know for whom the bell tolls; it tolls for thee."

The teaching of the Bible concerning death is this. When the body dies, the soul lives on. The body is not the most important part of us; the soul is. Someone has computed that if we were to analyse the amount of chemicals in our body – salt, magnesium, phosphate, potassium, etc., the actual worth of those chemicals in money terms would be very little, perhaps no more than a few pounds. The soul, however, is of inestimable worth. One New Testament scripture puts it like this: "What shall it profit a man if he gain the whole world and lose his own soul?" The soul which is the non-physical part of us – the part we know as "personality" – will live on either in close relationship with God or apart from God. If the soul is the most important part of us, doesn't it make sense to give as much attention to it as we do to our weight, our blood pressure and so on?

One of the greatest and most-loved sections of the Bible is Psalm 23. Here it is:

The Lord is my shepherd, I shall not be in want. He makes me lie down in green pastures, he leads me beside quiet waters, he restores my soul. He guides me in paths of righteousness for his name's sake. Even though I walk through the valley of the shadow of death, I will fear no evil, for you are with me; your rod and your staff, they comfort me. You prepare a table before me in the presence of my enemies. You anoint my head with oil; my cup overflows. Surely goodness and love will follow me all the days of my life, and I will dwell in the house of the Lord for ever.

Knowing God in the way the psalmist knew Him is the secret of overcoming death. When the time comes to pass from this world we need to know that God is with us in the "shadow". I have sat at the death bed of many people in my time, but I have never heard one say, "I wish I had spent more time on my business, or education, or amassing a fortune." What those who know they are dying usually say is, "I wish I was better prepared for this." Would you like to know God in such a way that gives you confidence as you face death?

The good news is – you can.

CHAPTER FIVE

WHAT IS THE ANSWER?

Unbelievable though it might sound to some, there is an answer. It is possible to have the deep thirst of one's heart fully satisfied. Five considerations are looked at in relation to this, and the way to life – real life – is explained.

WHAT IS THE ANSWER?

I made the point earlier, but I want to make it yet again, that however difficult some may find it to accept, there is just no way one can find true meaning or fulfilment in this life and have the assurance that all will be well in the life to come without entering into a personal relationship with God. He made us, and He made us for Himself. As St Augustine put it some fifteen hundred years ago on the first page of his famous *Confessions*: "Thou hast made us for Thyself, and our heart is restless till it finds its rest in Thee."

Why is it that when faced with this inescapable and sublime truth something rises within us to resist it? I have been leading people to an understanding of spiritual things for over four decades now, but I never cease to be astonished at the fact that when people are confronted with the reality of the things I have been discussing in this book, a tremendous struggle seems to go on in their souls.

I have thought long and hard about this and I think in the main there are two things that account for it – fear and pride. There are few words as confusing as "pride". The dictionary defines it in two ways – as "self-respect" and "arrogance". It is the latter meaning I am concerned with now. Pride is believed by many theologians to be the root of all sin. When analysed carefully, any sin can be seen as the result of a desire to be the centre of our world.

I have seen many people recoil in unbelief when I told them that pride is the desire to be God, because few have an awareness of a desire to dethrone God. We may not be aware of that desire, but believe me the principle of pride that lurks in your heart and mine is capable (potentially at least) of turning God out of the very universe He made. When St Augustine was asked in the fourth century what he considered was mankind's greatest malady, he gave the answer in one word – pride.

Pride (if we let it) can soon persuade us our place is to be the ruler rather than the subject. This is God's world and we are His creatures. He built us that we might have a relationship with Himself, but our pride has led us to believe that we don't need God and that it would be the greatest indignity to have to bow the knee to Him. Pride can even tell us that we are too intelligent to believe there is a God or, if we do believe, it can prevent us asking His forgiveness for the wrongs we know we have done.

Fear contributes to our problems too. The fear of being honest, for example, and discovering a challenge that demands more of us than we are prepared to give. Fear is the reason we distort our real situations and clothe them in excuses and rationalisations. We are also afraid of the feelings of helplessness we might experience if we surrender our lives to God. One woman said to me on one occasion: "But if I give myself to God that will mean I will be at His mercy." She saw God as a dictator and a tyrant; someone who just wanted to have control over her. It was a caricature, of course, for if God wanted us to be His slaves rather than His children, then He would have made us like machines, not as people with a free will. Pride and fear mingle together to produce a stubbornness in us that resists the most wonderful invitation mankind could ever receive – the invitation to know God and enter into a deep personal relationship with Him.

We need God if the ache in our souls is to be satisfied – that's the truth of it. The emptiness of our hearts will never be filled until they are filled with God. But how do we find God? How do we get to know Him?

Getting into a relationship with God is not essentially different from getting into a relationship with a human being. First there is the stage of drawing near. This is the tentative, explorative stage. Then there is the second stage – the stage when there is a desire to give yourself to the other person – the stage of decision. The third stage is when you actually give yourself to the other person and there is a mutual exchange of the selves. The stage of commitment. You belong to the other person and the other person belongs to you. From then on, there is a continuous mutual adjustment of mind to mind, will to will and being to being, down through the years. If this is the way to know another human being, should it surprise us if this is also the way to know the greatest Person of all?

There are those, of course, who say they will not believe in God or give themselves to Him until He proves Himself to them. What they reveal by that statement is their lack of awareness of the elements of relationship. "Prove Him to me," someone said to me on one occasion, "and I will believe in Him." But God cannot be "proved" in the sense that a mathematical formula can be proved. The mistake this person made was to suppose that logic or some system of experiments worked out on a laboratory bench is the only way to knowledge. There are many things we know which have not been proved (or cannot be proved) in terms of logic.

Some things we know by intuition and need no one to prove them to us – that kindness, for example, is better than unkindness and that the truth is better than a lie. Some things we know by experience, like the security that flows down deep inside us as a result of our mother's love. The only way to *know* another person is not by logic, mathematical systems or laboratory experiments, but by venturing upon a relationship.

Whenever anyone asks me to help them find the path that leads to God there are usually five things I share with them. These can be seen as five steps that, when considered and acted upon will bring us into a relationship with God. First, I tell them to *keep in mind that the initial step towards spiritual reality and satisfaction is complete honesty*. This is very easy to say, but much more difficult to grapple with. The business of being really honest in all things is difficult, even painful, and more so than we usually realise.

I encourage people to see that this is the moment for complete candour. I invite them to face the fact openly and honestly that there is an ache within them that up until now they have been unable to meet. I say to them, "Tune in to that fact, for pretending it isn't there gets us nowhere." The words of Simone Weil, which I quoted earlier, are very powerful and to the point:

> The danger is not lest the soul should doubt whether there is any bread, but lest by a lie, it should persuade itself that it is not hungry. It can only persuade itself of this by lying, for the reality of its hunger is not a belief but a certainty. [26]

All our lives it has been easier for us to deny our ache for meaning that lies deep within us, for to admit it causes a level of pain to surface that is difficult to handle. But when we know that God is there, and that He waits to link Himself to our lives, the situation is quite different. The ache in our souls *can* be satisfied. God was the one who put the thirst within our souls in the first place, and He is the only one who can fully satisfy it.

I encourage people to ask themselves these questions: How have I handled this deep longing of my soul in the past? How hard have I worked to assuage my pain, to keep it out of awareness? Have I tried to fill up the emptiness with terrestrial things like activity, pleasure, drugs or striving for success? Where has it all got me?

I talked to one young man who admitted that his strategy for dealing with the pain of his unmet needs and his anxiety about the life to come was simply to kill the longings of his soul by not wanting. He said, "It is better to feel nothing than to allow my feelings to come into awareness and then not have them satisfied." He did not realise it, but his strategy for dealing with the pain of his unmet spiritual hunger helped him maintain a kind of equilibrium. But at what awful cost to his personality?

I always make the point also when talking to people about these issues that it requires great courage for them to face their pain. But I would not be a responsible spiritual advisor if I did not encourage them to do it. I read the other day of a young man who was taking his first flight on a plane. He looked extremely nervous, but when his companion asked him how he felt he said, "I'm fine . . . not a bit nervous." Minutes later he was sick all over his companion. It was easier for him to be sick than to face the fact that he was nervous. Facing the important questions that life thrusts upon us is often disturbing, but if we are to experience spiritual health, then face them we must.

The second thing I tell people is this: *understand that if you are going to receive the life of God into your soul then it must be received as a gift and not as a matter of human achievement.* The idea that the life of God is a gift to receive is difficult for some people to accept. There are two reasons for this. One is that they find it incredible that the great God of the universe would concern Himself with the needs of earth-born creatures like ourselves. I have heard the point argued in this way: "With such a tremendous universe to control and millions of galaxies to supervise, how can it be conceived that the great God and Creator would take an interest in the personal details of our lives?"

But God has told us in the Scriptures that He watches every one of us and cares for us with a Father's love. Jesus Christ said that God cares so much for His created universe that a sparrow cannot fall unnoticed to the earth. And then he added: "You are worth more than many sparrows" (Matthew 10:29–31).

The other reason why some have difficulty in accepting the life of God as a gift is because it offends their pride to be told that they can do nothing to earn God's interest or attention. There is something in our personality that would like to merit it, or earn it. This panders to our pride. So humility – the opposite of pride – is demanded here. But we are afraid to be humble because of the implicit threat to our pride. Yet without this humility we separate ourselves from the very remedy we seek.

I must be frank and say that there is just no way anyone can earn God's approval. Men and women of the most rigorous morality have tried to do it in every age, but they have always failed. There is no road to God that way. Does that mean that morality and goodness are not as important as we have been led to believe? No, they are extremely important and are highly commended everywhere in the Scriptures. It's just that morality and goodness *in themselves* are not the things that bring us to God.

If we are to have the life of God enter our souls and to taste the aliveness which our hearts so desperately crave, then we must receive it as a gift; it simply cannot be earned. I know that this affronts many, for they feel they would like to be able to do something to merit it. This is why so many are drawn to those kinds of religions that encourage human achievement. They cannot see that their efforts to earn God's favour are really a way of pandering to their pride. The Bible spells it out in the clearest of terms:

> For it is by grace [God's unmerited favour] you have been saved, through faith – and this not from yourselves, it is the gift of God – not by works, so that no-one can boast (Ephesians 2:8).

The gift of life that God offers us, however, does not come without cost. In fact it cost God the death of His Son upon a cross. Ever wondered why Christians make so much of the cross, why it decorates so many churches? It is because on that first Good Friday Jesus Christ, God's Son, died in order to pay the price for our sins.

I have found in talking to people over the years that the very mention of Christ's death on the cross triggers a string of questions such as these: How could the death of one person, even though He was the Son of God, atone for the sins of everyone in the world? How could He die for *my* sins if nineteen hundred years were to pass before I committed any? Why do I need a Saviour at all? Couldn't God just forgive us without His Son having to go to a cross?

I am not addressing these questions in this book, but let's just concentrate for a moment on the real issue that lies behind the cross. Something happened through Christ's death on the cross that made it possible for God to forgive us our sins, and enable Him to approach us with the offer of the gift of life. Two thousand years ago, Jesus Christ cleared the debt of sin that was against the human race on that Roman gibbet in such a way that makes it possible for us to come to God and receive forgiveness for our sins.

A priest by the name of Peter Green tells how he came out of his church in Salford one day and saw a young working man staring incredulously at a crucifix. Seeing the priest, the young man said: "I don't see what good it done the Father that His Son should die like that." But it wasn't for the good of the Father that Christ died; it was for the good of sinners such as you and me. Sin demands punishment in any righteous world and God's Son bore the dreadful cost. This is one of the most central and glorious truths of the Christian faith – that God bent to mankind's dilemma and did for us what we could not do for ourselves.

When we insist on doing something to earn God's offer of life, we by-pass the work which Christ did on the cross. We push aside God's appointed way of salvation and prefer one of our own. Can you see the arrogance that underlies this attitude? It is tantamount to spitting in the face of the Almighty and saying, "I don't like your way; I prefer my own." Such an attitude, as I am sure you can see, gets us nowhere. So let there be no talk about earning God's approval. God's offer of life is not something to be achieved, but something to be received. It is a gift from God.

The third thing I tell people who want to find God is this: *recognise that the only way to know God is through his Son, Jesus Christ.* Many respond to this by saying, "But aren't there many different paths to God? What about the many different religions and different experiences that people talk about in relation to their search for God?" I explain that though it is true that there are many paths that lead to God (different life experiences, for example), the only way to *know* God and enter into a personal relationship with Him is through His Son, Jesus Christ. This is in fact the message of the New Testament, and Christ Himself put it in the clearest of terms when He said:

I am the way and the truth and the life. No-one comes to the Father except through me (John 14:6).

Another question that people ask at this point is: "Where does this leave the other religions – the ones that are non-Christian? Isn't one religion as good as another?" I usually explain that there are fine things in most faiths. Christianity recognises these fine things and is grateful for them. But Christianity says:

In the past God spoke ... at many times and in various ways, but in these last days he has spoken to us by his Son, whom he appointed heir of all things, and through whom he made the universe (Hebrews 1:1–2).

Note this is not simply Christianity's claim – it is *God's* claim that Jesus Christ is God's last word to the world. This might sound arrogant and exclusive, but based on what God says, Christianity is not one religion among others. It is in a category by itself. It contains not just the word of a prophet, *but the word of the Son of God Himself.*

No other world faith has claimed that its greatest teacher was God incarnate. The word "incarnate" is one term used by theologians, which means "God in human form". It staggers people when they first hear Christians claiming that Jesus Christ is God incarnate, but it is true nevertheless. Archbishop William Temple, one of the greatest archbishops this country has ever known and who died just after the Second World War, used to say that no one had a right to believe in the Incarnation who had not first found it incredible.

Christianity is not just a religion of influences and values and principles; it is that, but it is much more than that. It is a religion of happenings, of events, of historical occurrences, of facts. Indeed, one of the greatest facts is this – God came to us at a certain hour in history in the form of a baby (the first Christmas) and at a certain place on earth, ancient Palestine, lived and died among us and afterwards rose from the dead.

Why did God go to such a length as to enter this world in human form? The truth is that we could never find God by searching for Him, so He had to come and find us. All religions teach mankind's search for God, but the Christian religion emphasises God's search for us. This is why the Christian faith is often referred to as "gospel". The word "gospel" means "good news". Consider with me now why that is so.

Other religions say that you have to climb the ladder of worthiness and self-effort rung by rung, and maybe one day you will find God at the top. Christianity turns that idea on its head and says that you do not find God at the topmost rung of the ladder of worthiness and self-effort having climbed it rung by rung. You find Him at the bottom of the ladder because He has come down the ladder of the Incarnation right to where we are. If this is not good news then I don't know what is! All the non-Christian approaches to God emphasise moralism and striving to be worthy of God's interest and attention through techniques, thought forms and various methods of austerity. Once again it is humanity's proud attempt to lift itself to God rather than accept the fact that God has come down to us.

It is popular nowadays for people to reassess Jesus Christ, but almost all of those who write about Him are full of admiration for His character. The writer Anthony Burgess said: "If God's like Jesus, God's worth believing in." And the dramatist Dennis Potter describes Him like this:

There's this Man striding around in an occupied territory, knowing, and then not knowing that he is going to die and to die painfully. And in the middle of it all to say things that have never been said and are still not said about love. As a model of what human behaviour can be like it still stands supreme. [27]

Christianity says that Jesus Christ whom so many admire and applaud is actually God in human form. Listen to these actual quotations from the Bible (a few among many):

No-one has ever seen God, but God the One and Only, who is at the Father's side, has made him known (John 1:18).

Anyone who has seen me has seen the Father (John 14:9).

The Son is the radiance of God's glory and the exact representation of his being (Hebrews 1:3).

The Word [Jesus] became flesh and made his dwelling among us. We have seen his glory, the glory of the One and Only, who came from the Father, full of grace and truth (John 1:14).

You will notice that in the last text quoted Jesus is referred to as "the Word". This term, perhaps more than any other, enables us to grasp just how it is that Christ is able to reveal God to us.

As you have taken hold of my words in the pages of this book, so you have taken hold of my thoughts. If I had left these pages blank and hoped you might guess my thoughts, then even if you had actually purchased a blank book it would have been a fruitless exercise. How can you get hold of my thoughts unless you first get hold of my words? When you listen to Christ and focus on His words, you are picking up the thoughts of God. If you want to know what God is like, look at Jesus. In a Sunday School class once I heard a little child blurt out: "Jesus is the best photograph God ever had taken." He is! We draw near to God in Jesus. There is just no other way.

The fourth thing I invite people to focus on is this: *consider that before your soul's ache can be truly satisfied you must find God's forgiveness for your sins*. Everyone has something for which they need to be forgiven. I have often been astonished at how unforgiven sin in a person's life can lead to all kinds of mental, emotional and even physical distress. A psychiatrist friend of mine puts it like this: "I am convinced myself that what underlies the problems that bring people into counselling or psychotherapy is unresolved guilt."

Time and time again I have traced the roots of people's problems back to what psychologists call "a conscience distress", but what is really best defined as "an old sin". There is really no way known to psychology for radically dealing with a conscience distress. A skilful counsellor or psychiatrist can dig it out from the labyrinths of a person's mind, can dangle it in front of them, but he or she is powerless to forgive. Only God can forgive sins. That was how people first began to suspect that Christ was God on earth. He forgave sins!

But let us be quite clear as to the sin that needs to be forgiven. It is possible to ask God to be forgiven for such sins as lying, stealing, fornication, adultery, bitterness, lust, self-pity, ingratitude, hatred, thoughtlessness and so on, but to let the central sin remain. The sin that has to be identified – the *central* sin – is the sin of independence. By this I mean the desire to go our own way rather than God's.

I draw a distinction myself between the words "sins" and "sin". "Sins" I see as those things I have listed above, but "sin" is the stubborn and arrogant desire to undertake a declaration of independence in relationship to God and live and act (even though we may not say so) as if He did not matter. Sin is really a state of alienation from God; the fact that we are distanced from Him and choose to remain distant from Him. It is this commitment to independence that must first be recognised, confessed and repented of if God is to come in. The other sins must be brought before Him too, but no revolution can take place in the soul until we recognise that our desire to remain free of God's involvement in our lives is the core issue. When we face that, confess it and tell God we are sorry about it, then the forgiveness of God will flow in.

You can come to God with perfect confidence that your sin can be forgiven, for the Bible gives this promise:

If we confess our sins, he [God] is faithful and just and will forgive us our sins and purify us from all unrighteousness (1 John 1:9).

No one can be truly happy until he or she is forgiven.

The fifth and final step I encourage people who want to know God to take is this: *open your whole being to God and surrender yourself into His hand.* Remember what we said earlier – there can be no real relationship between two people without the inward commitment to one another. If either one withholds the essential self from the other, then the relationship is blocked. God is ready to commit Himself to you. Are you ready to commit yourself to Him?

When we give the one thing we have to God – ourself – then we have the right to accept the very thing God has to give to us – Himself. Many fail at this place, for they give themselves to God, but fail to receive. Suppose two people did that in a marriage situation – gave themselves to each other, but did not receive from each other – the marriage would never get off the ground.

Listen to how the Bible puts this point:

> Yet to all who received him [Christ], to those who believed in his name, he gave the right to become children of God (John 1:12).

It is at this point that I explain something else that is an essential part of the Christian message – faith. This is a term that is often misunderstood. Many people think of it in the same way as the schoolboy who when asked to define it said, "Faith is believing what you know to be untrue." That is not what faith is all about. Faith is simply *trust*. The word implies a form of belief, but faith at its heart has an attitude of trust. It is the venture of the whole personality in trusting one who is worthy of that trust.

We use faith every day of our lives. When we board a train we have faith that the driver knows his job. When we go to a restaurant for a meal we have faith that the food is wholesome and well cooked. A lot of our business arrangements are conducted on the basis of faith too. The very word "credit" is simply the Latin form of "trust". If faith is to be found in all our human relationships, should it surprise us to find it in forming a relationship with God?

Now permit me at this stage to talk directly to you. Are you conscious of an ache deep inside you that has never been satisfied? Are you aware also that inside you are weaknesses, dark problems and sins that you have never been able to deal with? You feel you need the help of someone else if your life is to be made whole. That Someone is as close to you as the breath you breathe. As you open up your life to God you will experience the good news that the first disciples carried everywhere in the first century and their true followers have echoed in every century since.

The time has come now to venture on God, to give yourself to Him, and for Him to give Himself to you. Remember, however, that you must *want* to do it. God will never bludgeon His way into a person's life and will never intrude where He is not welcome. The first step must be yours. God has done everything to make it possible for you to know Him, and now it is up to you. As you confess your sin, His love and forgiveness will flow into your soul. When you ask, you will receive.

For close on 2,000 years men and women have been doing this and have known God come in and transform them. It is not as though you are the first; millions have done it before you. So venture now on Him. You need no human intermediary to come to God. If you think it will help, seek out a minister of a Christian church, but remember you do not *need* an intermediary. No one is further than one step away from God and that one step is turning round. When you do, you will find yourself in the arms of a seeking God.

If you would like to surrender your life to God, then a special prayer has been prepared to help you do this. Find a quiet spot where you will be uninterrupted. Sit, stand or kneel – whichever is preferable – and pray the prayer sincerely and from the bottom of your heart. Prayer is simply talking to God in your mind or in audible words. It is best, whenever possible, to pray aloud. There is something about hearing the words you are saying which helps to reinforce them in your heart.

A PRAYER OF COMMITMENT

"You will seek me and find me when you seek me with all your heart." (Jeremiah 29:13)

O God my Father, I come to You now in the name of Your Son, Jesus Christ. Thank You for revealing Yourself to the world through Him, and for what He did on the cross to pay the price for my sin.

You have made Yourself known to me and, as I sense Your presence on the threshold of my soul, I want to open the doors of my inner being and let You in. I want to surrender my life into Your hands.

I make this choice understanding the implications. I know how not to live. I want to learn how to live – with You.

Forgive me for resisting You for so long. Forgive me for my stubbornness and my independence. As I turn to You I ask for humility of heart and mind, knowing that, as I reach up to You, You are reaching down to me.

Cleanse me from every sin. Give me the assurance that You have accepted me – that I am Yours and You are mine.

Help me to live a life worthy of You. Give me the strength to tell others of my new relationship with You. Guide me through every day. I am no longer my own – I belong to You.

I ask all this in the name of Jesus, Your Son, and my Saviour.
Amen.

As a record of the day and hour in which you received Christ, you might like to complete the following. Keep it safe. It is a reminder of your commitment to the Lord Jesus Christ.

Today, the   of   20
I committed my life to Jesus Christ and received Him into my life as Saviour.

Signature

WHAT HAPPENS NOW?

If you have made the decision to turn your life over to God, you have settled the greatest issue that can ever confront a man or woman in this world. Now that you have committed yourself to Christ you will find a growing assurance in your heart that you are His. There are several things you need to do, however, in order to develop this new life.

First, tell someone – like a close friend – that you have become a Christian. They may not understand all the implications, but you will be surprised how talking about this commitment will deepen your own awareness of what you have done.

Secondly, if you are not attending a Christian church, try to join one as soon as possible. God is pleased when His children meet together, and it is important for you to find a church where you are comfortable with the style and form of worship, where the Bible is clearly taught and where you can talk to the minister or leader and tell him that you have recently committed yourself to Christ. While all Christian churches believe in God and practise the Christian faith, they have different customs, and it may be helpful to visit a few churches in your area before deciding which one you would like to settle in.

Thirdly, plan to spend some time every day (or at least regularly) reading the Bible and talking to God in prayer.

These are the spiritual exercises that will help you grow and develop as a Christian. My booklet *Every Day with Jesus for New Christians* consists of daily readings for two months. I will be glad to send you a free copy if you write to me at the address below.

May God bless you in your daily walk with the Lord Jesus Christ.

Selwyn Hughes

Special Ministries
CWR
Waverley Abbey House
Waverley Lane
Farnham
Surrey GU9 8EP
England

NOTES

1. Quoted by Alister McGrath in *Bridge Building: Creative Christian Apologetics* (Inter-Varsity Press, 1992) p20.
2. Carl Jung, *Modern Man in Search of a Soul* (Kegan Paul, 1933).
3. Harold Kushner, *When All You've Ever Wanted Isn't Enough* (Simon & Schuster, 1986).
4. W.E. Sangster, *Why Jesus Never Wrote a Book* (Epworth Press, 1932), p79.
5. John White, *Greater Than Riches* (Inter-Varsity Press, 1922), p93.
6. Malcolm Muggeridge, *Chronicles of Wasted Time* (Collins).
7. C.S. Lewis, *The Weight of Glory* (Macmillan, New York).
8. Diogenes Allen, *The Traces of God* (Cowley Publications, 1981), p19.
9. *Oxford Book of English Verse* (Oxford University Press).
10. Carl Jung, *op. cit.*
11. John White, *op. cit.*, p25.
12. William Watson, "World Strangeness" in *Selected Poets* (Thornton Butterworth 1928).
13. Source not traced.
14. Simone Weil, *Waiting for God* (Putnam, 1951), p210.
15. M. Scott Peck, *The Road Less Travelled* (Rider & Co, 1985).
16. *Ibid.*

17. *Ibid.*

18. C.S. Lewis, *The Problem of Pain* (Collins Fontana, 1940), p81.

19. Anthony Clare, *In the Psychiatrist's Chair* (William Heinemann, 1992), p218.

20. *Ibid.* p219.

21. David Dempsey, *The Way We Die* (McGraw-Hill, 1977).

22. Source not traced.

23. W.E. Sangster, *These Things Abide* (Hodder & Stoughton).

24. Quoted by Hans Hoffman in *The Official Register of Harvard University* (25 April 1958).

25. Frederick Treeves, *The Elephant Man* (Cassell, 1928), p176.

26. Simone Weil, *op. cit.*

27. Source not traced.

NATIONAL DISTRIBUTORS

UK: (and countries not listed below)
CWR, Waverley Abbey House, Waverley Lane, Farnham, Surrey GU9 8EP.
Tel: (01252) 784710 Outside UK (44) 1252 784710

AUSTRALIA: CMC Australasia, PO Box 519, Belmont, Victoria 3216. Tel: (03) 5241 3288

CANADA: CMC Distribution Ltd, PO Box 7000, Niagara on the Lake, Ontario L0S 1JO.
Tel: 1800 325 1297

GHANA: Challenge Enterprises of Ghana, PO Box 5723, Accra. Tel: (021) 222437/223249
Fax: (021) 226227

HONG KONG: Cross Communications Ltd, 1/F, 562A Nathan Road, Kowloon.
Tel: 2780 1188 Fax: 2770 6229

INDIA: Crystal Communications, 10-3-18/4/1, East Marredpally,
Secunderabad – 500 026. Tel/Fax: (040) 7732801

KENYA: Keswick Bookshop, PO Box 10242, Nairobi. Tel: (02) 331692/226047
Fax: (02) 728557

MALAYSIA: Salvation Book Centre (M) Sdn Bhd, 23 Jalan SS 2/64,
47300 Petaling Jaya, Selangor. Tel: (03) 78766411/78766797 Fax: (03) 78757066/78756360

NEW ZEALAND: CMC Australasia, PO Box 36015, Lower Hutt. Tel: 0800 449 408
Fax: 0800 449 049

NIGERIA: FBFM, Helen Baugh House, 96 St Finbarr's College Road, Akoka, Lagos.
Tel: (01) 7747429/4700218/825775/827264

PHILIPPINES: OMF Literature Inc, 776 Boni Avenue, Mandaluyong City.
Tel: (02) 531 2183 Fax: (02) 531 1960

REPUBLIC OF IRELAND: Scripture Union, 40 Talbot Street, Dublin 1. Tel: (01) 8363764

SINGAPORE (DIRECT CUSTOMERS): Campus Crusade Asia Ltd, 315 Outram Road,
06–08 Tan Boon Liat Building, Singapore 169074. Tel: 222 3640

SINGAPORE (BOOKSHOPS): Armour Publishing Pte Ltd, Block 203A Henderson Road,
11-06 Henderson Industrial Park, Singapore 159546. Tel: 276 9976 Fax: 276 7564

SOUTH AFRICA: Struik Christian Books, 80 MacKenzie Street, PO Box 1144,
Cape Town 8000. Tel: (021) 462 4360 Fax: (021) 461 3612

SRI LANKA: Christombu Books, 27 Hospital Street, Colombo 1.
Tel: (01) 433142/328909

TANZANIA: CLC Christian Book Centre, PO Box 1384, Mkwepu Street,
Dar es Salaam. Tel/Fax: (022) 2119439

USA: CMC Distribution, PO Box 644, Lewiston, New York, 14092-0644.
Tel: 1800 325 1297

ZIMBABWE: Word of Life Books, Shop 4, Memorial Building, 35 S Machel Avenue, Harare.
Tel: (04) 781305 Fax: (04) 774739

For email addresses, visit the CWR website: www.cwr.org.uk

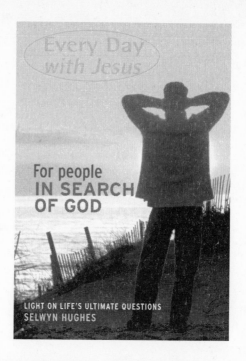

LIGHT ON LIFE'S ULTIMATE QUESTIONS

Every Day with Jesus for People in Search of God is a great tool for friendship evangelism, answering, clearly and thoughtfully, all those demanding questions that people often struggle with. Selwyn Hughes offers an intelligent perspective on life's big issues, including:

* What is life all about?
* Who is God and what is He like?
* Why does God allow suffering?
* Is there life after death?
* How can I know God?

PRICE: £1.99
ISBN: 1-85345-226-2

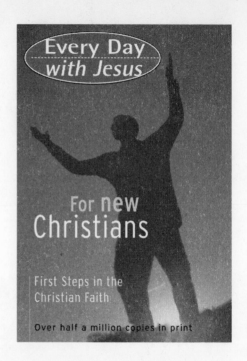

Every Day *with Jesus*

For new Christians

First Steps in the Christian Faith

Over half a million copies in print

FIRST STEPS IN THE CHRISTIAN FAITH

Every Day with Jesus for new Christians is a powerful and relevant handbook for people new to the Christian faith. A favourite with churches of all denominations, with over half a million copies in print.

PRICE: £1.95
ISBN: 1-85345-133-9